Whisper on My Palm

Whisper on My Palm

*Poems in a Time of Grief, Illness,
and a Global Pandemic*

Sarah Agnew

RESOURCE *Publications* • Eugene, Oregon

WHISPER ON MY PALM
Poems in a Time of Grief, Illness, and a Global Pandemic

Copyright © 2022 Sarah Agnew. All rights reserved. Except for brief quotations in critical publications or reviews, no part of this book may be reproduced in any manner without prior written permission from the publisher. Write: Permissions, Wipf and Stock Publishers, 199 W. 8th Ave., Suite 3, Eugene, OR 97401.

Resource Publications
An Imprint of Wipf and Stock Publishers
199 W. 8th Ave., Suite 3
Eugene, OR 97401

www.wipfandstock.com

PAPERBACK ISBN: 978-1-6667-3675-5
HARDCOVER ISBN: 978-1-6667-9552-3
EBOOK ISBN: 978-1-6667-9553-0

JANUARY 7, 2022 11:47 AM

Contents

Acknowledgements | vii

CRISIS
we were all there | 3
Choking | 4
Touch | 6
M*A*S*H | 7
lament of the chronically fatigued vicar | 8
Reverberation | 10
Last Christmas | 11
The rawest cry | 13
together: enough | 15
Diary of a Chronically Exhausted Vicar. Episode 34 | 17
with | 18

CONNECTED
fall, water | 23
On the healing nature of green | 24
found | 26
long after : loves | 27
Tucked in | 28

Cheese Night | 29

lockdown gratitude | 31

lunch time | 32

Like a brave green shoot | 33

it's funeral day | 35

Bereft

without him | 39

waking | 40

grief upon grief | 41

the same | 42

undone | 43

Hold this | 44

life without our fathers | 45

The pine cone that picked me up | 46

and remember | 47

all my tears | 48

All you can grieve | 49

Eighteen | 50

Lonely

still the flame | 53

breathless | 54

Depression | 55

a day improved | 56

I, kintsugi | 57

Solitary

I am not a mother | 61

follow the leaf: three ways to dwell in love | 63

sacred solitude | 64

Acknowledgements

MY THANKS TO FELLOW POETS who read the draft manuscript of this collection and made wise suggestions for small changes that made significant improvements: Michelle Coram, Katie Munnik, Andrew Wright. And to my mum, as always.

'Sacred solitude' was first published on artandtheology.net, 31/10/2019; 'The rawest cry' was first published on arthandtheology.net, 26/06/2020. Reprinted with permission.

I am grateful to Sharon Hollis for her commissioning of a poem through the #WritersForFireys donation campaign in 2020. Inspired by her theme of 'dwelling in love', I composed 'long after: loves', and 'follow the leaf: three ways to dwell in love'. Other poems have been inspired by people close to me, and I am grateful to you.

Many of the poems in this collection were first published online on my former and current blogs. sarahagnew.com.au

Crisis

we were all there

in response to the stories told of a man with a knife in central Sydney, 13 August 2019

it wasn't me cut with the knife
he thrust into the crowd
and we all bleed

it wasn't me they found alone
in the flat around the corner
and life diminishes for us all

it wasn't above my head
on my car he trampled
and we are all frightened

it wasn't me raging and flailing,
incoherent, mad
and we are all lost

it wasn't me that pinned
him down to protect us
and we all find our humanity again

Choking

A lament for Australia, Summer 2020

Where do we begin
with this great wall of fire
or that fire storm
or the hungry angry monster?
Where do we begin?

How do we enfold them all
into our love, the dozens
of humans dead, the hundreds
of homes razed, the thousands
of folk displaced, the millions
of acres burned, the billions
of creatures dead—how can
our embrace include them all?

What is the starting point
for our care, now, this task
now to rebuild: which lives
to prop up, which towns to
reconstruct, which roads to open,
what first? what next? what do we do?

We need You.
We need You here with us,
and with us all. We need
courage and wisdom, love
and compassion; we need
safety, we need care, we
need healing, we need hope—
O, Holy One, we need You.
Draw us in, fill us up,

send us and go with us as we reach
out from where we are, one step, one
act, help us remember we are
one, and to find that somehow, thus,
we have begun.

Touch

I cannot hold your hand today,
friend or stranger, when we meet.

I take instead the rose's leaf,
"hold me," it said,
"offer me your greeting."

I cannot share embrace with you,
kin or neighbour, in love and gratitude.

I reach instead towards the sun,
"come near," it beckons,
"receive from me this kiss."

I cannot pick you up today,
young child in the circle of my care.

I play instead with dirt and earth,
"carry me," the plants request,
"to new soil in which to grow."

M*A*S*H

I started in the late '90s,
watching re-runs in the early
evening, recording episodes to VHS,
watching those when the show
went off air for a while; later, I
collected eleven series on DVD,
watched episodes with lunch to stretch
tired eyes between hours at the books
and screens, studying, proofing,
writing; stretch muscles for
laughing, crying, raging at the ravages
of war; and how they danced,
little more than a shuffle
and a sway, a hug to music (like
us that one, messy night, oh,
delight), in tents and their Mess
holding on, holding on, holding
on to each other, to sheer life,
close and vulnerable and touched

lament of the chronically fatigued vicar

my people are gathering
and I am not with them;
the congregation together,
I on my own

your people will join
their voices in praise,
confess our collective turning away,
receive your welcome, your grace

your servant will sigh
her stilted praises,
reaching for joy, yearning for peace,
searching for you, alone

your people will sing
the Sacred Story,
hear it, proclaim it, commit
again to enact it, together

your servant will honour
your Story, her story,
in stillness
and the small piercing silence

my place with my people
stands empty today;
though another will speak,
only I can be me

the cost—the cost!
I count, and lose;
the gift, the gift
I would claim, I would

Oh Holy One,
hear my cry!
ease my pain,
help me remember

your people, as they gather—
you are with them;
though I am absent,
you are here

Reverberation

When all the lights are out
the stories of the day begin to echo
in the empty space, to awaken
stories held within and
then—then—the pieces of me pull
away from their rough patches
to be gathered in the shroud
around my being.

Last Christmas

For Christmas 2019 and 2020 (and the rest)

Last Christmas gave us
a fright, lines of dazzling light,
searing wounds visible
from highest skies.

This Christmas, we can not light
even small flames in wreaths
on unscorched tables, before still
smouldering lives.

Last Christmas gave us
the world's worst nightmare
shut down, too many
taken down by one small virus.

This Christmas we cannot fly
as far away or as close
as we would be, but have
learned again how love transcends.

Last Christmas gave us
first Christmas with, and the last;
first Christmas without, and
the last—

This Christmas our hearts
have healed a little, broken
more; and even grown open to new
lights that shine.

For last Christmas, past
Christmas, for this Christmas
and Christmas yet to come, for
Christmas, for Christ born again
and always, always, we say
Amen.

The rawest cry

for the caring professionals

When I hold your hand
on the crisp white sheet,
I pray with all my heart
for you—deep peace.

When I'm at home,
there's no one's hand
holding mine,
and mostly I'm just fine—

but maybe—maybe—
maybe I'm too strong
for my own good?

When I catch your tears
in frothy coffee remnants,
I pray with all my heart
for you—new hope.

When I close the door,
I pour my own wine
to catch my falling tears,
and most days, that's just fine—

but maybe—maybe—
maybe I'm too strong
for my own good?

When black dogs and monsters
cast clouds across the sun,
I pray with all my heart
for you—be well.

Then, at last, my dog wakes,
pulls me into the shadows;
and no one hears the rawest cry
that I am far from fine—

and maybe—maybe—
maybe I am too strong,
too strong for my own good?

together: enough

we held a zoom morning tea for our congregation this morning. it was wonderful. it was enough, and it was nowhere near enough, of a connection as we long to gather again.

twenty five screens connected
forty five faces smiling to see
each other, forty five
voices "hello"ing, laughing, sighing;
cups and mugs, biscuits and cakes:
it's the same, but so unusual.

twenty five rooms beamed
into twenty five homes,
not the forty or fifty lingering
in the foyer of our shared home:
we're still together, but we're still alone.

forty five stories of gifts
we receive in this season:
connection and presence through
the separation; learning,
slowing, healing, creating—
much we do not want to lose
when we regain what we have lost.

twenty five screens, twenty
five homes, forty five threads
holding us together—forty five
of the hundreds of our kin
seeing, seen; hearing, heard;
weaving these threads from this
connection to hold us

forty five heads bowed,
one voice for all, one prayer
with all, one Spirit we call
on you to stay, to hold,
to keep us all

Diary of a Chronically Exhausted Vicar. Episode 34*

I see the cringe as I rise
from my two hours' sitting—
"are you OK?"
"I am in pain"
"if there was only more
that we could do . . . "

I hear the cry of boredom,
your "waiting for death to come"—
I want to apologise,
I am not there;
if there was only less
need for me to be sorry.

I feel the water hold me,
bubbles gently soothe,
encourage me to move,
I am so weary;
if there was only more
that I could do.

---

* From a series of blog posts on sarahagnew.com.au

with

we need more "with"—
sitting beside and listening,
standing beside and supporting,
opening arms in welcome:
we need more "with".

we need longer tables
and more plates;
broader dance floors—
more dancing.
we need more "with".

and we need more love:
eyes open to see,
blinking with our weeping;
reaching out and holding hands:
we need more love.

we need kinder hearts
and broader smiles,
open doors,
lower fences.
we need more love.

we need
more compassion:
more us,
more "thank you";
more we,
more "welcome";
more together,
more "you matter";

more we differ
and that's brilliant;
more you differ
and that's a gift;
more together,
more "you matter";
more us,
more "with",
more love,
more compassion.
we need
more
compassion.

Connected

fall, water

for Mary Oliver, January 2019

this one this wild this
full abundant precious cup:
life overflowing

On the healing nature of green
after reading Phosphorescence, *by Julia Baird*

1. "I see trees of green"
as I read her reflections
on light in the dark,
on the healing to be found
in nature;
the experts she cites,
whose research uncovered
healing for folk who see green
every day;
I look

to my right where my pot plants
bask in the morning sun
through curtains I leave open
for them, in case I sleep in;
the next window along frames
the bush of magenta and gold roses,
no longer adorning branches of rich
dark green leaves;
looking ahead past kitchen,
over dining table and chairs,
or further left across the sofa
strewn with cushions and cross stitch
canvas and threads—

bushes, trees, leaves of every
shade of green are all
I can see;

later, when the sun moves around
I will take her book to the papasan
chair on the porch, my turn
to bask in sun light and green,
accompanied by the bees who love
the red flowery branches screening
my outside nook.

All that green, I see;
all the green they say
will heal,
and yet—

and yet, I am still

2. Well enough.

Remember the words of another,
writing to you, I speak gently
to myself;
the words of wonder as you fight
to live life as fully as you can,
as you achieve, and create,
though you pay some heavy price?

Remember the words used
to describe your quiet,
lonely hero's journey through each long day—
remember?

And I look again to my pot plants,
the bushes and trees, all that
green and I gush gratitude: for what
part they must play in carrying
this lonely heroine through her days,
I can but wonder,
in awe.

found

I met him too soon,
before I knew myself,
before I had learnt how to live
with the black dog
in my corner—and
the paradox, when I did
learn, the way for me was
solitude

he returns to me in dreams,
now, when alone turns
to lonely
we sit
side by side in silence as we
often did, as I wonder why
here is where he has chosen
to be, as I often did

then he takes my hand
and I am not alone;
we nestle close and once
again I am home and I close
my eyes again to return
to embrace I cannot find,
awake

long after : loves

1.

her favourite painting
above your bed, because she
let you choose, for your birthday

2.

your gasp—and smile—at
his ghost in her reflection,
tying your daughter's hair

3.

his "no regrets: you were
a gift, we were a gift"—
your two hearts works of kintsugi

4.

watching the game with empty cup,
his fountain of knowledge
no longer flowing

5.

warm rivers cascading down
deserted cheeks, again:
still dwelling in love, remembered

Tucked in

these clean flannelette sheets smell
like the cupboard in which they sat
through the warm months, waiting,
and remind me of her house—
not her sheets, for they were stored
in the taller cupboard on the other side
of the wall—but of her house, and thus
of her. this cupboard sat in the entrance
hall beneath the art deco mirror, facing
art deco glass front doors off the art
deco semi-circle porch—remembering,
now, I understand my favour for that era.
my sheets have the smell of the wood
my grandfather worked into the cupboard
that sat in the hall of the house up the hill
from the beach, and kept her telephone
books and odd pieces of paper,
and held on top the big fancy sea
shells my uncle brought back
from the desert—one came to me when
she left the house that has not
yet quite left me

Cheese Night

for Andrew, Jules, Emily, Grace, and Bethany

the next day I stand on the creaky
kitchen floor washing glasses
now empty of the bubbles boozy
and benign; mugs stained by the tea
to start the afternoon with shortbread
and chocolate; wine glasses, too, for
the first game, and the rule change
for the next round to less
ruthless rules from your house;
I remember we were subdued,
unusual, needing time to unwind
the stories coiled in heart strings
used to singing to each other from
afar, in these times of social distance

next the plates we filled at games'
intermission, from boards I also
wash this morning, last night replete
with Leicester, Goats, and Double Brie,
almond apricot soft cream
and hummus, olive, sweet
potato dips we scooped up on celery,
carrot and cucumber; I brush crumbs
of bread and corn chip, soak spoons
of their fig and pomegranate relish,
or onion caramalised; turn to find
the popcorn bowl—and more glasses!
Port and Bailey's, for the post-
dinner game that was new to you
and harder, but by now
at last the laughter has unfurled

and we proclaim on music
and partners and dystopian
novels that can stay or leave
the bookshelf, thank you!

now alone in the kitchen, detergent
bubbles all but vanished, I will eke
beloved cheese night further into this
new day with left-overs for lunch.

lockdown gratitude

this week, I am
grateful that when I needed
to get out of the house—
and I mean,
needed
to get out
of the house,
breathe, move, feel
the sunshine on my back and break
the shackles of lockdown
monotony, the sun
did push the clouds aside,
and the trees and plants and grass, too,
were stretching for it, were
singing with life after the rain and oh,
how I breathed again, and felt
like myself again

lunch time

bottle green broad brim hats bob
above the fence line,
above yellow shirts and green
shorts; a similarly incidentally patriotic
ocean behind them spreads
across oval and playgrounds beneath
winter's shining canopy.
as the blue car approaches, two
hands wave high and I
throw my left hand across the passenger
seat in a wave big enough to reach
them, and with sideways glance
catch their bouncing delight, splash
it across my face and—sigh—day
made!

Like a brave green shoot
Burns Night hope, 2021

Oh my hope is like a new green shoot
that's reaching for the sun.
Oh, my hope is like a dancing tune,
I'm bound to come undone.

It's rare enough to hope, I know,
rare in days like these:
for all the seas run dry it seems,
all the wells and all the dams.

But oh, my hope's a purple rose,
a yellow coat, a poem;
oh, my hope's an ancient song,
and the people—can you hear?—they're singing!

It's rare enough to hope, I know,
rare in days like these:
for the space from red and blue these days,
it's far, so far between.

And oh, my hope's a mourning song,
the land's lamenting sighs;
oh, my hope is standing strong:
get up, Australia, rise!

It's rare enough to hope, I know,
rare in days like these:
for our nation, built on theft and lies,
we've some dirt out of which to rise.

Oh, my hope is a new face mask,
some gloves and sanitiser, please!
Yes, my hope is in solitude,
though to be fair, it always was . . .

But it's a rare old hope, and strange, I know,
to hope in days like these;
yet, like that brave green shoot, I will
still stretch, and reach for the shining sun!

it's funeral day
for Rachel, and Maureen

Holy One, if
I could give her my courage,
you know I would;
if I could somehow ease
her aching, I would do
that, too—but
I can only sigh
the solidarity of a daughter
grieving a parent far too soon—
too soon—
and trust that you are
with her in her hour
of need, this new raw grief,
weeping—
and yet,
rejoicing
to welcome home
your daughter;
oh, Holy One,
Amen.

Bereft

without him

As engines roar and the nose
lifts, I am still waiting for
the voice over the cabin:

*Passengers, we apologise
for this delay, but we
return, for one to disembark—
they were mistaken, all is well.*

They will come to me and whisper,
*and you will pay the price,
you said, anything, you said,
everything, you vowed.*

Of course, I will say, yes, I will
say—take it, take it all; I can
give it up so readily because I
do not need to. I can not buy
back the way things were.

The wheels will not touch
down, the clock will not
reverse, the plane will fly me
home, will fly us on, without him:
it will all
go on

waking

I do not find mornings easy.
Dragging myself away
from slumber, where I have
been in a state of rest,
in subconsciousness,
been some blissful kind of free—
is an arduous ritual each
and every time.

Mornings are the hardest,
since he died.
Dragging myself into
this unwelcome new reality,
the memory of his absence,
the surreal truth: he is gone—
is an arduous ritual each
and every time.

grief upon grief

the tears came today,
of course, interrupting
breakfast, of course—
not yesterday
           with its space
           its solitude
           its freedom;
but today as I prepare
for the office, for
the weekly chat in his
or my office to share
the load the joy the
sorrow
           not yesterday's
two month anniversary
of the other loss
the bigger loss the deeper
loss but today
when grief cannot have
my attention, must not
pull me away from the life
I must keep living, the work
I will be doing now alone

the same

unrecognisable
landscapes one character removed
always—never

undone

they did not marry to fix
a brokenness, it was not
to complete the incomplete,
no, their wholes they brought
together to make something new,
a two—and that, not she,
is what is now incomplete, now
broken, now half what they
together had become.

Hold this

Hold this, says Life,
this package deal,
this need to heal
from deeply Tired and Blue.

Hold this, says Life,
this box of grief,
this loss of team
for now, for time unknown.

Hold this, says Life,
this tonne of grief,
this weight, this empty
screaming: father's absence . . .

life without our fathers
for Michelle

sit beside me in my grief*
you asked, in that moment that your
world changed as we never want,
ever hoping against inevitability—and I
answered from that ancient kirk with prayer
and poem, lit a candle on the page
with colours of friendship and of sorrow,
sent the answer far
across the oceans then between us—how
far it has travelled now, with you, and on
along with other promises of presence given
and received; but never has it ventured
deeper than today when my own words
returned, uttered in your answer to my
grief in the moment my world changed
as we never wanted

---

* "Sit beside me in my grief", *The Only Constants,* Adelaide: Ginninderra Press, 2016

The pine cone that picked me up

I picked up a pine cone today,
the gaps between the branches
of this mini Christmas tree all
full of needles; I held it and I smiled,
for the first time glad
of the transportation back to Dad and my
childhood and our expeditions into the forest
at the university where he worked and we grew up;
there where he and I were together,
our whole family connected
through the mortar, as bricks that built that place;

though for Mum its corridors are overrun with shadows
of mistreatment: of my Dad and now
my sister; and before, her Dad; for me
the shadows on the plaza, in the tavern,
where I met my love and lost him
have since receded with welcome light;
and though the forest has its ghosts of souls that leapt
in sorrow—not a method I considered—today

I am connected to my story through
the pine tree's seed, and I remember
childhood forays to gather spindly wicks
for the hearth of our warm home—oh, and grand
whispering overseers of his mother's home
in her pocket of Scotland nestled
into South Australia—and today
it didn't hurt to lift my eyes,
to look into the memories, held
in a fallen pine cone

and remember

sometimes
in my dream my Dad
is still alive

then I wake up

all my tears
For Dad

I cry with Fatigue,
and I am crying for you

I cry, inflamed muscles aching,
I am crying for you

I cry anger at isolation,
but find: I cry for you

I cry another grief altogether,
but these tears are for you

I cry at the Black Dog stirring,
and I am crying for you

I cry, homesick, for family,
and of course, it's for you

I cry at the weight I carry alone,
but the tears are for you

I cry over nothing at all,
I am still crying the loss of you.

All you can grieve

we're tasting seconds now
in this buffet of grief life served up:
your granddaughter's second
birthday without you,
middle daughter and wife's, too;
your grandson's second
Christmas, our second without you.

it's the fifth time I
have come home to no
you, and in my seasonal
playlist "The Little Drummer
Boy" played as we flew
over Hindmarsh Stadium descending
toward the runway, as if
I needed reminding

it all still tastes sour,
of course, but we're adapting,
keep helping ourselves to
more, returning
to the table and its gaping
empty seat

Eighteen*

Even now,
it's as if no time at all has
gone. But you
have. You have; and
the space gapes a void with no hugs or your laughing
eyes, mischief dancing there, love singing there.
Even now,
no time at all.

* 18 March 2021. Eighteen months since Dad died, 18/09/2019

Lonely

still the flame
life with chronic fatigue

I swam to move the muscles:
still, the flame raged.

I soaked to loose the muscles:
still, the flame raged.

Spa jets to soothe the muscles:
still, the flame raged.

I stopped,
I slept,

I let the muscles rest—
and yet

breathless

1.

yesterday the ocean rose,
towering dragon foaming at the mouth:
I rode the back of it,
sailed the length of it—

today it swallowed me

2.

yesterday the wind howled,
huffing wolf blowing down the house:
I turned my back to it,
swayed and bent with it—

today it shattered me

3.

yesterday the fog descended,
frightened fowl's wings smothering:
I leaned my back to her,
took my rest with you—

today she went too far

Depression

it's like a blank screen waiting to begin
it's like a python squeeze of my whole being
it's like I'm absent from my self

it's sadness with no memory of the cause
it's boredom with no desire for bounce
it's internal bruising, bloodless bleeding
it's an ache through to the bones
without having run a tangible race

it's facing a battle with no will to fight,
and no blade or breastplate if you did

it's sitting in the chair for hours alone,
immobile, dumb, un-remarking

a day improved

was it the seed planted
by my healing guide,
we're here again,
Sarah, will you not believe,
Sarah, you can be well?

was it the treat granted,
slivered almonds and sugar
spattering the floor with joy;
or the work crafting
dreams and prayers, sharing
the load repairing the broken?

was it the medicine at last
taken that eased the ache
that freed the body, freed
the strength all tangled in
chains of my own making?

I, kintsugi

once healed and whole again, but
fragile and back in the fray again,
without armour to deflect arrows,
without barricades for defence,
without clear sight of intended marks;

no strength to stand firm,
no reflex to duck punches,
no calm voice or wise words;

all I have left to me is retreat
lest the barbs land, or the beats strike,
lest the gold fail and I break again

Solitary

I am not a mother

*in response to Mothers' Day—speaking for myself,
and happily.*

I have brought much
to life—poems, stories,
books and dreams,
but I am not a mother.

I nurture, guide, encourage
humans to their flourishing
with love and presence, for
I am big sister,
I am aunt,
I am mentor,
I am pastor, prophet, priest:
but I am not a mother.

Oh, I bleed, with painful
tedious regularity,
the body holding possibility;
I will not partner,
neither to coax possibility
to conception, nor to
step into, adopt,
the mother-load,
for I am not a mother

by choice,
for life—the life that sees
me thrive and nurture
life in many ways,
as woman, as human,

as member of community, but
not "mothering": that day
is not for me.

follow the leaf: three ways to dwell in love
for Sharon

veins connect through stem
and branch lifeblood pulls you home
takes what you receive

wind catches, carries
mysterious embrace draws
you into the dance

flutter on river
slow and hurry bubbles you
into life with all

sacred solitude

I had thought the tangible empty
the tingling hint the yearning
for palm to palm—an absence
but I begin to feel a whisper
Your whisper across my palm
where no other hand will fit,
no other can remain,
in intimate embrace.
others feel Your grasp in
the clasping hands with an other, but I—
am I destined for a different
kind of intimate?

not sex not tawdry not "in love
with God My Saviour"
this taking hand in hand
this different
I have known much longer
than admitted
without name without voice
for what was clouded before
the forced withdrawal this fogged
fatigue demanded cleared
the way and now as once before
in darkness here we are
here with me You are here
the only one I never
turn away and is that not
the intimate, are You not
the one to hold my hand, the one
who will bear witness, and it has taken
me till now to truly shed

the story I've been told
that in that place can only
stand a human?

I hear another story:
Hildegard, Julian, Thérèse
tell me another story of being one
whose hand is held by
Holy hand—and by no other
tell me now my story so that I
can feel the whisper
on my palm as Presence.

www.ingramcontent.com/pod-product-compliance
Lightning Source LLC
Chambersburg PA
CBHW071748040426
42446CB00012B/2498